Vicksburg Battlefield
Monuments

Vicksburg Battlefield
Monuments

Vicksburg Battlefield Monuments

A Photographic Record

Photographs by Harold Young
Text by Steve Walker and David F. Riggs

UNIVERSITY PRESS of MISSISSIPPI   Jackson

Library of Congress Cataloging in Publication Data
Young, Harold.
  Vicksburg battlefield monuments.

  1. Vicksburg National Military Park (Miss.)—Pictorial
works. 2. Vicksburg (Miss.)—Siege, 1863—Pictorial
works. 3. Soldiers' monuments—Mississippi—Vicksburg
National Military Park—Pictorial works. I. Walker,
Steve, 1950–   . II. Riggs, David F.   III. Title.
E475.27.Y68   1984   973.7′344   84-7386
ISBN 0-87805-214-3 (pbk.)

Contents

Acknowledgments

Manuscripts, documents, architectural drawings, and other materials in the Vicksburg National Military Park archives were the major sources for this publication; additional details were obtained directly from the monuments. Several individuals deserve a special word of thanks for their assistance to this project. From Vicksburg National Military Park this includes Albert P. Scheller, whose knowledge of the Vicksburg campaign and park has been invaluable to staff and visitors alike for more than a decade. C. Bowie Lanford, the park's chief of interpretation, and Kay Boolos, business manager for Eastern National Park and Monument Association, proposed the book and served as the park's liaison with the publisher. Edwin C. Bearss, chief historian of the National Park Service and the authoritative source on the Vicksburg campaign and the park's history, reviewed the manuscript and made perceptive recommendations. Gordon A. Cotton, director of the Old Court House Museum in Vicksburg, furnished the early photographs of park monuments and ceremonies which are extracted from the museum's J. Mack Moore Collection. Reference material and pertinent articles from the *Vicksburg Evening Post* were provided by Susan A. Riggs of the Warren County-Vicksburg Public Library. And, for their courteous editorial assistance, we wish to thank JoAnne Prichard, Barney McKee, and Hunter Cole of the University Press of Mississippi.

Vicksburg Battlefield
Monuments

Here brothers fought for their principles;
here heroes died for their country;
and a united people will forever cherish the
precious legacy of their noble manhood.

Here Brothers Fought

When Vicksburg's grayclad defenders surrendered to Gen. Ulysses S. Grant's Union forces on July 4, 1863, virtually every soldier and sailor present recognized the importance of the event. Over 140,000 men had struggled for possession of the Southern stronghold and, when it fell after a daring campaign that culminated in a forty-seven day siege, it split the Confederate states in half and restored Northern control of the Mississippi River.

Situated on a 200-foot bluff overlooking a bend on the Mississippi side of the river, Vicksburg withstood its first test when Adm. (then Flag Officer) David G. Farragut failed to capture the city with naval vessels during the spring and summer of 1862. Army efforts to construct a canal and divert the river likewise failed. But the North needed the Mississippi River for unrestricted shipping of troops and supplies, and this last stretch between Vicksburg and Port Hudson, Louisiana, was all that remained in Confederate hands. Southerners were determined to defend it, however, because Northern control of the river would sever Texas, Arkansas, and most of Louisiana from the rest of the Confederacy.

In October 1862 three men whose roles were influential in the struggle for Vicksburg assumed key positions. General Grant was appointed commander of the Department of the Tennessee, and Adm. David Dixon Porter took charge of the Mississippi Squadron. Together Grant's army and Porter's navy set their sights upon unrestricted access to the river, which meant the capture of Vicksburg, the strongest fortified point. Opposing them was Gen. John C. Pemberton who became commander of the Department of Mississippi and East Louisiana that same month.

During the winter of 1862–63 several Union efforts to capture Vicksburg failed. Grant, who marched toward the city by a northern land route, was compelled to retreat when his supplies were destroyed by Gen. Earl Van Dorn's cavalry at Holly Springs in December. Later that month Gen. William Tecumseh Sherman, who travelled southward by river and disembarked just north of Vicksburg, was repulsed with 1,800 casualties while inflicting only 200 at Chickasaw Bayou, ending the two generals' combined effort. The remainder of the winter and early spring was spent in futile operations collectively known as the Bayou Expeditions. These efforts did, however, serve a purpose. The public's demand for action was eased, the Confederates were kept guessing about Grant's plans and, equally important, the Union troops were toughened by the hard work and maintained the spirit of the offensive.

Late in March Grant started to move his army of approximately 45,000 men southward on the Louisiana side of the river and gathered his forces near Hard Times, below Vicksburg. On the night of April 16 Porter successfully passed Vicksburg's river batteries with eight gunboats and two transports; five more transports followed them six nights later. As his intentions to cross the Mississippi became more obvious, Grant created two diversions. Sherman was ordered to make a feint at Snyder's Bluff north of Vicksburg, and Col. Benjamin H. Grierson led a cavalry raid from La Grange, Tennessee, to Baton Rouge, Louisiana. Grierson destroyed Confederate communications and supplies and, more importantly, captured the attention of Confederate cavalrymen who chased the blueclad horsemen and ignored Grant.

When Porter's gunboats were unable to capture Grand Gulf, Grant moved further south and crossed the Mississippi, landing at Bruinsburg on April 30. After a victorious fight near Port Gibson on May 1, Grant moved northeastward and defeated Southern troops at Raymond on May 12. Two days later the Federals defeated Gen. Joseph E. Johnston at Jackson and captured the state capital. Then Grant's army turned westward toward Vicksburg. Pemberton's forces met him at Champion Hill on May 16, the largest confrontation between the two antagonists thus far, and were defeated with 3,900 casualties for the Confederates and 2,400 for Grant. The following day Pemberton was defeated at Big Black Bridge and retreated to his fortifications at Vicksburg. The Union army approached the city on May 18.

Flushed with five successive victories and believing that the Confederate morale had been shattered, Grant attempted to capture Vicksburg by storm. An attack on the Stockade Redan failed on May 19 with lopsided losses of 900 Northerners and 100 Southerners. Undaunted, Grant launched an even larger assault force on May 22 but it, too, failed, this time with casualties of 3,200 attackers and 500 defenders.

President William McKinley rode through the arch at the former entrance to Vicksburg National Cemetery during a visit on May 1, 1901.

Construction progress on the Illinois memorial as of November 1, 1905, by the Culver Construction Company of Springfield, Illinois.

Convinced that Vicksburg would not fall easily, Grant besieged the city. Pemberton's defenses—nine strong points connected by a line of trenches—were nearly nine miles long and were manned by 32,000 troops. Grant's army hemmed in the grayclads by land while Porter's gunboats joined the bombardment from the river and made the encirclement complete. The Confederates were unable to obtain reinforcements, food, or ammunition, and many of the city's beleaguered citizens took refuge in caves to escape the shelling. Meanwhile the Federals dug thirteen approach trenches and steadily moved closer to the Southern lines.

In contrast to Pemberton's desperate situation, Grant's numbers swelled to 77,000 men. Many of these soldiers were assigned to the Union army's exterior line. These troops guarded the rear of Grant's investment line against Johnston's army of relief which was organized to relieve Pemberton but failed to act in time.

During the siege the Federals detonated mines under the 3d Louisiana Redan on June 25 and July 1, but these efforts were unable to overcome the defenders. Nonetheless, the Confederates were weakened physically by six weeks of strenuous resistance. Constant shelling, insufficient food, and exposure had taken a severe toll.

Pemberton, who recognized the hopelessness of his situation, met Grant between the lines on July 3 to discuss surrender terms. At first Grant insisted upon unconditional surrender which was unacceptable to Pemberton. Subordinate officers eventually proposed satisfactory terms, and on July 4 the Vicksburg garrison surrendered. More than 29,000 of Pemberton's men signed paroles not to fight again until exchanged. This included 5,900 men who were in hospitals, two-thirds of them afflicted with disease. The Confederates also had suffered 9,000 casualties since Grant had begun his campaign on March 29; Union casualties were 10,000. In addition Grant's army captured a large quantity of war materiel. Five days after Pemberton surrendered, Port Hudson also fell to Federal forces.

Dedication of the Mississippi memorial on November 13, 1909 (note that the memorial was incomplete; bronze work was added three years later).

Old Court House Museum

Northern control of the Mississippi River was complete. The river was open to commerce and the Confederacy had been split in two. President Abraham Lincoln triumphantly declared, "The Father of Waters again goes unvexed to the sea."

Union forces took the first step toward commemorating the campaign with erection of a monument in 1864 that marked the site where surrender terms had been discussed. But when veterans assembled at the Blue and Gray Reunion in 1890, momentum gathered to set aside the battlefield permanently. In 1895 the Vicksburg National Military Park Association formed and made its objective the establishment of a federal park. In 1899 they were successful.

For more than three decades the park was administered by the U. S. War Department. During this period William T. Rigby served the longest tenure as resident commissioner and was responsible for efforts to mark and restore the battlefield. Approximately ninety-five per cent of the Union memorials and markers were erected by 1917, and most of the Confederate monuments were placed after World War I. A veterans reunion in 1917, known as the Peace Jubilee, was the occasion for many memorial dedications. Elaborate ceremonies were typical whenever state memorials were dedicated.

More than 1,200 memorials mark Vicksburg National Military Park. Twenty-eight states had units in the Vicksburg campaign, and all but Kentucky and Tennessee are represented by memorials. In most instances the individual states funded their own memorials as well as state monuments and position markers. Federal funds financed most busts, relief portraits, statues, and the blue Union and red Confederate iron tablets. Heavily represented among the sculptors whose work is displayed throughout the park is the husband and wife team of Henry Hudson and Theo Alice Ruggles Kitson who created seventy-eight works between them.

Most monuments are placed where the units served. Those located in the area of Grant's headquarters are an exception, however; units represented in this northeastern section of the park served either in Louisiana or in Grant's exterior line which guarded his rear. Portions of Confederate Avenue that are outside the park boundary represent members of Gen. Joseph E. Johnston's army of relief, which never reached Vicksburg, as well as units which served in that area. Approximately 150 cannon, mostly original tubes with replica carriages, mark many artillery positions.

In 1933 Vicksburg National Military Park was transferred to the National Park Service, U. S. Department of the Interior. It stands now in silent tribute to the combatants who fought for possession of the city known as the Gibralter of the Confederacy.

Old Court House Museum

The 1st Regiment, Illinois National Guard, at their state memorial's dedication ceremony on October 26, 1906 (Shirley house to right in background).

Wisconsin dedicated its memorial on May 22, 1911, the forty-eighth anniversary of U. S. Grant's second assault upon Vicksburg. His son, Maj. Gen. Frederick Dent Grant, was present at the ceremony.

A team of oxen, shown here on Vicksburg's Jackson Street in 1903, hauled the fifteen-ton boulder which served as the base for the Massachusetts memorial.

On November 14, 1903, Massachusetts dedicated the first state memorial in the park.

Ninety-foot high observation towers stood near the Illinois memorial, Fort Hill, and the Maryland memorial. Completed between 1908 and 1910, eventually they became safety hazards and were leveled between 1963 and 1965.

State Memorials

Alabama

Dedicated in 1951, the Alabama memorial rests upon a base of Stone Mountain (Ga.) granite. It is located on ground defended by Gen. Stephen D. Lee's brigade, composed of five infantry regiments and an artillery battery from the Heart of Dixie. Seven embattled soldiers and a woman are grouped around a Confederate flag. According to sculptor Steffen Thomas, the flag represents the spirit of Alabama which never failed, for it was supported by men and women alike. The men are portrayed as defenders of Southern ideals, their homes, womanhood, and the spirit of Alabama; the woman is a poignant reminder that, while husbands and sons were absent, women maintained their homes and kept the spirit of Alabama uplifted. "This woman," the sculptor insists, "is Alabama herself."

Arkansas

In quiet dignity the Arkansas memorial stands "to the Arkansas Confederate soldiers and sailors, a part of a nation divided by the sword and reunited at the altar of faith." Dedicated in 1954, the memorial was constructed of Mount Airy (N.C.) marble by William Henry Deacy. A central shaft splits the memorial and bears a bronze sword mounted like a cross which represents the divided nation, but it is reunited on the "altar" that contains the dedicatory inscription. The state seal is affixed to the sword's hilt. A relief on the left panel depicts the Arkansas infantry in battle. Appropriately, the right panel bears a relief of the ironclad ram C.S.S. *Arkansas* which valiantly defended Vicksburg in July 1862.

ARKANSAS

TO THE ARKANSAS
CONFEDERATE SOLDIERS
AND SAILORS A PART OF
A NATION DIVIDED BY
THE SWORD AND REUNITED
AT THE ALTAR OF FAITH

Georgia

Unlike most states, which dedicated their memorials to all their sons who participated in the campaign, Georgia devoted her memorial to the Georgians who died at Vicksburg. Accordingly the memorial resembles a cemetery monument. The gray granite shaft, which stands approximately eighteen feet high and exhibits the state seal, was dedicated in 1962. It is identical to Georgia memorials at Gettysburg and Antietam and bears the solemn inscription:

We sleep here in obedience to law;
When duty called, we came,
When country called, we died.

Illinois

Illinois had more participants in the Vicksburg campaign than any other state. One of her adopted sons, Abraham Lincoln, was president of the United States during the Civil War while another, Ulysses S. Grant, was among the foremost generals and commanded the Union army at Vicksburg. Appropriately the Illinoisans erected an impressive memorial.

A commission of war veterans selected a site along the Jackson Road, a vital point in the siege line, for their monument. Groundbreaking ceremonies were held in 1904 for the "Temple of Fame" which was the prodigy of Charles J. Mulligan and the architect, Maj. William Le Baron Jenney who was chief engineer for Sherman's XV Corps at Vicksburg; the cost was $194,423—a sizable sum in the early 1900s. Two years later the memorial was dedicated amid elaborate festivities. Preceded by an evening ball, a parade which featured the 1st Regiment, Illinois National Guard marched from the city to the completed memorial on October 26, 1906. The Prairie State's Governor Charles S. Deneen officially accepted the memorial from the commission and, in turn, presented it to the U.S. War Department.

The Illinois memorial is a combination of grandeur and symbolism. Modeled after the Roman Pantheon, it stands sixty-two feet high and fifty-four feet in diameter with an opening in the dome eleven feet in diameter designed to provide natural lighting. The circular exterior is etched with excerpts from Lincoln's second inaugural address and Grant's acceptance speech for his first presidential nomination, as well as eagles and shields placed alternately to represent attack and defense. Stone Mountain (Ga.) granite forms the base and stairway; above the base is Georgia white marble. There are forty-seven steps in the long stairway—one for each day of the siege of Vicksburg.

A portico supported by six Doric columns bears sculptures of three women who represent history recording the deeds of North and South. Above them is a bronze eagle with its outstretched wings above the reunited nation. Three panels with bas-relief busts of Lincoln, Grant, and wartime Illinois Governor Richard Yates top the memorial's entrance. Inside, a mosaic of imported marble composes the floor with the state seal in the center. The walls, which are Tennessee gray marble with Georgia white marble panels, are inscribed with the names of Lincoln, Grant, and other prominent officers. Especially unique are sixty bronze tablets which name all 36,325 Illinoisans who participated in the Vicksburg campaign.

Indiana

Oliver Perry Morton, one of the strongest wartime governors, is perpetuated in bronze as the Indiana memorial by sculptor George Brewster. Park commissioner Rigby suggested the statue, which was dedicated in 1926.

Iowa

Born on the day that Gen. Robert E. Lee surrendered at Appomattox Court House, Henry Hudson Kitson seemed destined to create Civil War sculpture. He produced nine sculptures for Vicksburg alone. Kitson selected Vermont white granite for the Iowa memorial. The Greek-Doric structure is semi-ellipsed with six bronze reliefs affixed to it. A bronze tablet in the middle with three reliefs on either side lists the Iowa units which served in the Vicksburg campaign. An equestrian statue of a standard-bearer is located centrally to the fore. The memorial was dedicated in 1906.

The six bas-relief panels depict successive engagements in the Vicksburg campaign. From left to right they represent the battles of Grand Gulf, Port Gibson, Jackson, Champion Hill, Big Black Bridge, and Grant's second assault against Vicksburg on May 22, 1863. This latter attack included a penetration of the Confederate lines by soldiers of the 22d Iowa at the Railroad Redoubt within sight of their memorial.

Kansas

Abstract symbolism is featured in the Kansas memorial, erected in 1960 and dedicated the next year as part of the Mississippi Civil War Centennial commemoration. Three circles represent the United States at different periods of history. The lower circle symbolizes the prewar nation, united and at peace. In the middle, a broken circle depicts the country divided during the Civil War. A whole, upper circle represents the reunited nation. An eagle, the national symbol, crowns the sculpture.

Louisiana

In 1887 a memorial to the Louisiana soldiers killed in defense of Vicksburg was erected downtown. Located in the rose garden on Monroe Street between South and Crawford Streets, this foreshadowed the numerous memorials yet to come. In 1902 Louisiana also became the first Southern state to select a site for a state memorial in the military park.

Appropriately, the Louisiana memorial is located on the Great Redoubt. It was here and at the nearby 3d Louisiana Redan that Louisiana troops defended the Jackson Road, an important entrance into the city which was near the center of the Confederate defense line. At 397 feet above sea level, this site is the highest point in the park.

The Louisiana memorial is an eighty-one foot high Corinthian column topped with a brazier and "eternal flame" constructed entirely of granite. On the front of the base is the state coat of arms flanked by Confederate battle flags; other sides of the base list the Louisiana units in the Vicksburg campaign. The memorial was designed by Albert Wieblen and presented to the U.S. War Department by the state's Governor John M. Parker during dedication ceremonies in 1920. Like the soldiers it honors, it stands guard over the surrounding hills.

Massachusetts

Vicksburg's citizens took notice when a fifteen-ton boulder was unloaded at the city's railroad siding, transferred to a large four-wheeled cart, and hauled by twenty oxen to the northeastern end of the military park. The cumbersome granite stone had been shipped directly from Massachusetts to serve as the pedestal for the state's memorial. Shortly thereafter a bronze statue of an infantryman was mounted upon the rock. Also affixed to the boulder was a plaque which bears the state coat of arms, the IX Corps badge, and a list of Massachusetts regiments in the Vicksburg campaign. Dedicated in 1903, it was the first state memorial in the park.

Theo Alice Ruggles Kitson, whose husband Henry also designed monuments for Vicksburg National Military Park, was the sculptress. Mrs. Kitson created an additional sixty-eight busts and relief portraits for the park.

Michigan

Herbert Adams carved the statue and lower third of the Michigan memorial from a forty-ton stone. The completed obelisk, which is thirty-seven feet high, is composed of Bethel white granite and bears a statue of the Spirit of Michigan at its base. It was dedicated in 1916 and stands near Battery DeGolyer, the largest concentration of artillery at Vicksburg, named for Samuel DeGolyer, the gallant artillery captain of the 8th Michigan Battery who was mortally wounded near this site.

Minnesota

A ninety-foot obelisk commemorates Minnesota's role in the Vicksburg campaign. Made of Mount Airy (N.C.) granite, sculptor William Couper placed a bronze statue of Peace at its base where she holds a sword and shield to signify that the soldiers of both armies have placed their weapons in her keeping. Bronze plaques on either side of the obelisk list the Minnesota units in the campaign, and the front of the structure displays the state coat of arms. The memorial was dedicated in 1907.

Mississippi

Of all the states to erect memorials at Vicksburg National Military Park, it is ironic that the state most reluctant to place a monument of any kind was the host state, Mississippi. When a bill was introduced in the state legislature in January 1906 to establish a monument commission, it met with opposition. A number of Confederate veterans were members of the legislature and they believed that it would be a shame and a disgrace for Mississippi to erect a memorial on federal property to commemorate a Union victory.

Because of the efforts of former Confederate Gen. Stephen D. Lee (who served on the military park's commission) the bill to create the Mississippi Vicksburg Park Memorial Commission passed the state House of Representatives by a vote of 68-46. After making a personal appearance to win the issue, Lee fought an equally strenuous battle to secure an appropriation. The problems of his poor health were compounded by developments in the debate which prompted him to write to Commissioner Rigby, "I am thoroughly disgusted with the attitude of my comrades in the Legislature." The appropriation issue finally was brought to a vote on February 7 with sixty-eight votes needed to pass, and Lee emerged triumphant, 68-51.

The memorial that the legislature funded was constructed by Frederick E. Triebel with Mount Airy (N.C.) granite and stands seventy-six feet high. Although it was dedicated in 1909, the bronze work had to come from Rome, Italy, and was not completed until 1912. Centrally located among the bronze Confederates, seated above the state coat of arms, is Clio, the muse of history. She is portrayed recording the names of Mississippi's sons on a roll of honor.

Missouri

Perhaps no state whose sons participated in the Vicksburg campaign better typified the horrors of the Civil War than did Missouri. Forty-two Missouri units participated in the campaign, twenty-seven Union and fifteen Confederate. This tragedy was remembered by the state's monument commission, which selected the very site for their memorial where two opposing Missouri regiments clashed in battle.

The Missouri memorial is unique as the only state memorial on the battlefield dedicated to soldiers of both sides. It is a forty-two foot high pylon (symbolic of the forty-two Missouri units) flanked by a fifteen-foot high wall. A bronze relief panel on the wall to the left of the pylon represents Union Missourians on the attack. A similar panel to the right depicts Confederate Missourians in defense. Sculptured between the two panels is a Roman galley bearing a bronze statue of the Spirit of the Republic on its prow. Above this figure is the state coat of arms.

Victor S. Holm sculptured the memorial of Missouri red granite, and it was dedicated in 1917 during the "Peace Jubilee." Park Commissioner Rigby discouraged the state's original recommendation for two separate memorials in order to foster the atmosphere of brotherhood and reconciliation which he sought to establish in the park. The memorial's inscription reflects this mood:

> *To commemorate and perpetuate*
> *The heroic services*
> *The unselfish devotion to duty*
> *And the exalted patriotism*
> *Of the Missouri soldiers*
> *Union and Confederate*
> *Who were engaged in the*
> *Campaign, siege and defense of Vicksburg*

New Hampshire

Erected in 1904, the New Hampshire memorial is composed of rough granite and stands approximately twenty feet in height. It bears the IX Corps badge (the corps in which all its regiments served), the state seal, and a list of New Hampshire regiments in the Vicksburg campaign.

New York

A forty-foot obelisk made of Mount Airy (N.C.) granite commemorates the role of New York troops in the Vicksburg campaign. A plaque on the front lists the units, and a comparable one on the back describes their activities. Circular plaques are attached to each of the memorial's four sides; the plaque on the front bears the state coat of arms, and (clockwise) the others represent the artillery, the IX Corps badge, and the infantry. (All New York units were either infantry or artillery in the IX Corps.) The memorial was dedicated in 1917.

Ohio

Rather than construct a single state memorial, Ohio chose to erect a separate monument for each of its thirty-nine units that participated in the Vicksburg campaign. Ohio's commissioners were directed to locate the site where each unit had fought in order to place the monuments on location. As the first representatives sent by a state to mark troop positions, the Buckeyes had to establish locations without the benefit of other state markers as references. Their first survey was conducted in 1901 and, though each man was a campaign veteran, the changes in topography during the intervening thirty-eight years complicated their task. By study and perseverance their work was completed late that year.

Ohio awarded the contract to construct the monuments to the Hughes Granite & Marble Company of Clyde, Ohio, which had provided satisfactory monuments for the state at Shiloh National Military Park. The monuments were dedicated in 1905.

Pennsylvania

After construction delays caused by a yellow fever epidemic in Vicksburg, the Pennsylvania memorial was dedicated in 1906. It consists of a granite shaft placed at the back of an eliptical platform approached by a flight of three steps. At the rear of the platform is a granite bench. The state coat of arms is on the platform's left side, and a IX Corps badge is on the right. Five bronze medallions on the main shaft portray each Pennsylvania unit's commander: (from left to right) Col. John I. Curtin, Lt. Col. Thomas S. Brenholtz, Col. John F. Hartranft, Col. Daniel Leasure, and Capt. George W. Durell. Each officer's name is inscribed beneath his portrait, and each man's unit is listed on the back of the memorial with the state coat of arms. The portraits were sculptured by Charles A. Lopez and the general monument design, selected from ninety-two entries, was the work of Albert Randolph Ross.

One of the most outstanding features of the memorial is the inscription above the five portraits. It succinctly expresses the reason for the preservation of the battlefield and the establishment of Vicksburg National Military Park:

> *Here brothers fought for their principles; here heroes died for their country; and a united people will forever cherish the precious legacy of their noble manhood.*

Rhode Island

A statue of a courageous infantryman in attack represents the 7th Rhode Island Infantry, the state's lone regiment in the Vicksburg campaign. The sculptured figure holds a rifle musket in his left hand and an upraised regimental flag, its staff shot away, in his right. Engravings of the state coat of arms and the IX Corps badge are on the back of the pedestal. Designed by Francis Edwin Elwell, the memorial was dedicated in 1908.

RHODE ISLAND
7ᵗʰ INFANTRY
COL. ZENAS R. BLISS
1ˢᵗ BRIG. 2ᴺᴰ DIV
9ᵗʰ CORPS.

Texas

When the Union army tried to shatter the Confederate lines at Vicksburg in a massive assault on May 22, 1863, they won a partial success at the Railroad Redoubt. But Waul's Texas Legion counterattacked and ousted the Federals from their toehold. The Texas memorial stands where this fighting occurred.

Constructed of Texas red granite, the memorial was created by Herring Coe and dedicated in 1961. It was completed two years later. Eleven steps leading to the bronze statue represent the eleven Southern states which seceded from the Union. The statue of the Confederate soldier captures the spirit of the Texans who sealed the breach in the Southern lines. A live yucca plant, native to the southwestern United States, is a unique addition to the memorial. An inscription on the left panel describes the fight at the Railroad Redoubt; on the right is a list of Texas units in the Vicksburg campaign. Inscribed on the memorial's center panel is a quotation from noted author John W. Thomason, Jr.:

> *Texas remembers the valor and devotion of her sons who served at Vicksburg and in other theaters of the War Between the States. For those men believed in something. They counted life a light thing to lay down in the faith they bore. They were terrible in battle. They were generous in victory. They rose up from defeat to fight again, and while they lived, they were formidable. The heritage they left of valor and devotion is treasured by a united country.*

West Virginia

After petitioning their state legislature on three separate occasions over a span of fifteen years, West Virginia veterans finally obtained funding for their memorial, which was dedicated in 1922. Sculptor Aristide Berto Cianfarani fulfilled the Unionists' wishes and mounted a bronze bust of Maj. Arza M. Goodspeed upon a pedestal of Rhode Island Westerly granite. Goodspeed, beloved by his Mountain State comrades, was killed in the assault of May 19, 1863.

Wisconsin

Early during the war a farmer presented the 8th Wisconsin Infantry with an eagle he had purchased from Chippewa Indians. The bird was adopted by the unit and named Old Abe for the president. The unit became known thereafter as the "Eagle Regiment." The soldiers carried Old Abe on a five-foot perch and in battle Old Abe would screech and beat its wings. When retired in 1864, the eagle was a veteran of forty-two clashes, including the Vicksburg campaign.

Presented to the state of Wisconsin, Old Abe was an honored resident in the state capitol until it died in 1882, weakened by noxious fumes which were mixed by a fire inside the building during the previous year. Then the treasured bird was mounted and displayed in the capitol until a second fire in 1904 destroyed its remains.

Today a six-foot statue of Old Abe stands atop the Wisconsin memorial to all soldiers from the state who participated in the Vicksburg campaign. The memorial was dedicated on May 22, 1911—the forty-eighth anniversary of Grant's second assault upon the city's defenses. W. Liance Cottrell was the architect and Julius C. Loester was the sculptor. The memorial stands a total of 122½ feet in height including the fifty-seven foot, six-inch-high granite column which supports Old Abe. Winnsboro (S.C.) granite was chosen for the memorial.

The platform for the tall column is enclosed on three sides by a four and one-half-foot-high wall. Mounted upon the inner side of the wall are bronze plaques which bear the names of 9,059 Wisconsin soldiers who served in the Vicksburg campaign. (Sixteen additional veterans were discovered later.) Bronze statues stand on either side of the wall; on the left side is a cavalryman, on the right, an infantryman.

At the base of the column are the Wisconsin coat of arms and three bronze reliefs. The relief on the right depicts a cannon in action; the one on the left shows a naval mortar crew. These two tablets combine with the two statues on the platform to represent the major branches of service at Vicksburg: the infantry, cavalry, and artillery of the army, and the navy. A third relief tablet at the rear of the column pictures a Union and Confederate soldier with hands clasped in friendship to symbolize the peace which exists now between North and South.

Florida

Constructed of Elberton (Ga.) granite, the Florida memorial was erected in 1954 by the United Daughters of the Confederacy to honor Florida soldiers who served in Gen. Joseph E. Johnston's army of relief. The front bears the state coat of arms and lists the Florida regiments in Johnston's army; the back features a brief inscription.

This memorial is outside the park boundary.

Maryland

This commemorative tablet to the 3d Maryland Battery, C.S.A., was erected in 1914 from private funds. The front bears a brief history of the battery; the back honors the memory of Captain Ferdinand O. Claiborne, who was killed during the siege.

This memorial is outside the park boundary.

North Carolina

The North Carolina memorial commemorates the service of Tarheels in Gen. Joseph E. Johnston's army of relief. It was sculptured from Stone Mountain (Ga.) granite by Aristide Berto Cianfarani and dedicated in 1925. An imprint of the state coat of arms accompanies a list of North Carolina regiments with Johnston.

This memorial is outside the park boundary.

South Carolina

South Carolinians who served in Gen. Joseph E. Johnston's army are honored by their state memorial, dedicated in 1935. Presented by the United Daughters of the Confederacy, it is constructed of Winnsboro (S.C.) granite. An engraving of a palmetto tree adorns the top of the memorial; below are a quotation from William Henry Trescot and a list of South Carolina units in Johnston's army.

This memorial is outside the park boundary.

Virginia

The Botetourt Artillery was the only Virginia unit to participate in the siege of Vicksburg. Its service is commemorated by a bronze tablet that was funded by private donations. Dedicated in 1907, it was the first Confederate tablet erected in the park.

This memorial is outside the park boundary.

Other Park Sites

Memorial Arch

In 1917 the U.S. Congress sponsored a four-day veterans' reunion at Vicksburg National Military Park with an appropriation of $150,000. Approximately eight thousand former soldiers attended the event. At its conclusion about $35,000 remained unspent, and the funds were used to commemorate the historic gathering. A memorial arch was designed by Charles Lawhon and constructed of Stone Mountain (Ga.) granite. Dedicated in 1920, it stood astride Clay Street until 1967 when, having been declared a traffic hazard, it was moved to its present site within the park.

Vicksburg National Cemetery

Established in 1866, Vicksburg National Cemetery is the burial ground for seventeen thousand Union soldiers and sailors who died in battle or from disease within a fifty-mile radius of Vicksburg during the Civil War. Among them rest thirteen thousand unknown soldiers. Tombstones with rounded tops usually designate identified graves; small square headstones mark the burial sites of unknown soldiers.

Shirley House

Known to Union soldiers as "the white house," the James Shirley family occupied this ante-bellum home in 1863. During the siege the Shirleys, who were Northern sympathizers, were removed to safety and their house was used as headquarters by the 45th Illinois Infantry.

U.S.S. *Cairo*

One of the earliest ironclads, U.S.S. *Cairo*, was the first warship sunk by a torpedo, or mine. *Cairo* was sunk north of Vicksburg in the Yazoo River in 1862 and raised in 1964. She has subsequently been restored in Vicksburg National Military Park adjacent to the *Cairo* Museum where artifacts from the gunboat are displayed.

Union Navy Memorial

Cooperation between the Union army and navy was a vital factor in their victory at Vicksburg. Adm. (then Flag Officer) David G. Farragut confronted the fortress city in May 1862 and learned that joint operations were a necessity. For more than a year the two services coordinated their efforts. Naval forces supported the bayou expeditions in the winter of 1862–63, escorted army transports, and protected army supply lines. Gunboats of Adm. David Dixon Porter's fleet passed Vicksburg's batteries on April 16, 1863, to a point south of town and on April 30 ferried the army across the Mississippi River from Louisiana. While Gen. U. S. Grant's army invested Vicksburg from the land side, the navy bombarded the city's Confederate defenders with approximately 12,000 shells.

The Union navy memorial is located at Battery Selfridge, the only land position manned entirely by sailors during the siege. Modeled after the Washington monument in Washington, D.C., it stands 202 feet in height and 20 feet wide on each of its four sides. Federal funds financed the memorial, and construction materials were furnished by the Woodbury Granite Company of Hardwick, Vt. Eight-foot-high bronze statues of four prominent naval officers surround its base. The statue of Porter, sculptured by Lorado Taft, faces the road. Proceeding in a clockwise direction from Porter the other statues depict Admirals Charles H. Davis, sculptured by Francis Edwin Elwell, Andrew H. Foote by William Couper, and Farragut by Henry H. Kitson.

Although it was completed in 1911, dedication ceremonies were postponed until 1917 when the park finally abandoned hope that a Confederate naval memorial would be constructed and the pair could be dedicated simultaneously.

Surrender Interview Site

When Generals Ulysses S. Grant and John C. Pemberton met to discuss surrender terms for Vicksburg they conferred beneath a large oak tree. Eventually souvenir hunters razed the landmark by chipping fragments for mementoes.

On July 4, 1864, the first anniversary of the surrender, Union occupation forces erected a monument to mark the surrender interview site. From a Vicksburg stonecutter's shop the soldiers obtained a marble shaft that had been intended to serve as a marker for Mexican War dead. Soon the shaft, too, fell prey to vandals, and in 1867 it was moved to the railroad depot and kept under constant surveillance. An iron 42-pounder cannon tube was set upright in the ground where Grant and Pemberton had parleyed. In 1868 the monument was relocated in Vicksburg National Cemetery. It remained there until 1940 when it was returned to its original location.

Grant Statue

ULYSSES S. GRANT, 1822–1885

A prominent general and United States president, Grant commanded the Union army at Vicksburg. His success in the campaign was one of his finest hours.

Frederick C. Hibbard, Sculptor, 1918

Pemberton Statue

JOHN C. PEMBERTON, 1814–1881

Ironically, this native Pennsylvanian commanded the Confederate army as lieutenant general at Vicksburg. After Vicksburg fell, Pemberton resigned his commission and served as a lieutenant colonel of artillery.

Edmond T. Quinn, Sculptor, 1917

Davis Statue

JEFFERSON DAVIS, 1808–1889

Despite earlier service in the U.S. Army, the House of Representatives, the Senate, and as Secretary of War, Jefferson Davis won lasting fame as President of the Confederate States of America. For years he lived in Warren County, Mississippi, south of Vicksburg.

Henry H. Kitson, Sculptor, 1927

Rigby Statue

WILLIAM T. RIGBY, 1841–1929

A captain in the 24th Iowa Infantry during the Civil War, Rigby made a lasting contribution through thirty years of service on the Vicksburg National Military Park Commission. He was the commission's chairman from 1902 until his death. Rigby was interred in Vicksburg National Cemetery.

Henry H. Kitson, Sculptor, 1928

Tilghman Statue

LLOYD TILGHMAN, 1816–1863

A brigade commander during the Vicksburg campaign, General Tilghman was killed at Champion Hill.

Frederick William Sievers, Sculptor

BRIGADIER GENERAL LLOYD TILGHMAN C.S.A.
COMMANDING FIRST BRIGADE OF LORING'S DIVISION
KILLED MAY 16 1863
NEAR THE CLOSE OF THE BATTLE OF CHAMPIONS HILL MISS

Vicksburg National Military Park

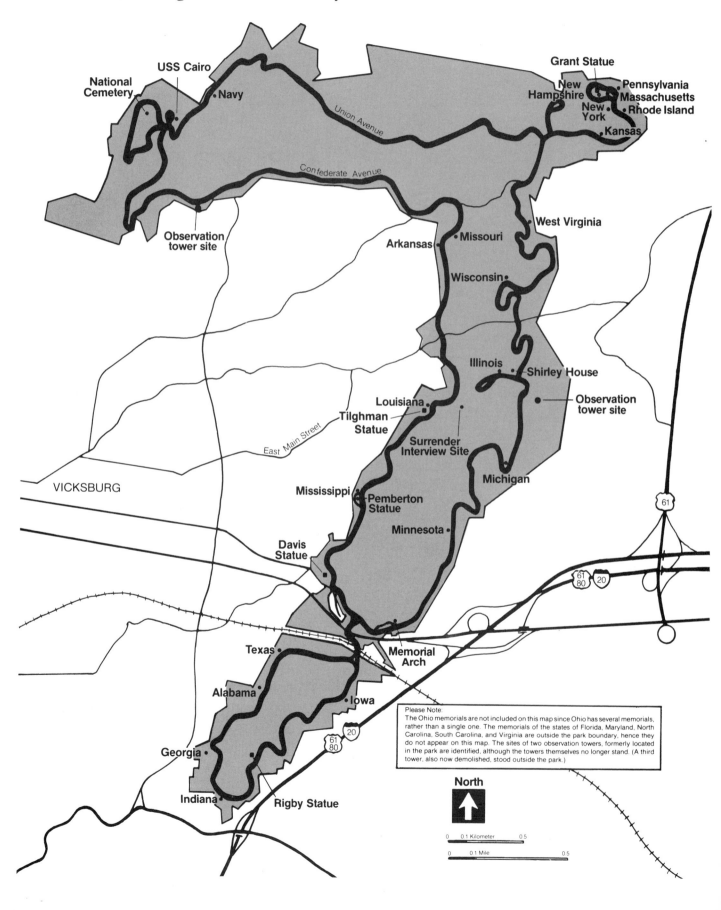

National Cemetery

USS Cairo

Navy

Grant Statue

New Hampshire

Pennsylvania
Massachusetts

New York

Rhode Island

Kansas

Union Avenue

Confederate Avenue

Observation tower site

West Virginia

Missouri

Arkansas

Wisconsin

Illinois

Shirley House

Louisiana

Observation tower site

Tilghman Statue

Surrender Interview Site

East Main Street

Michigan

Mississippi

Pemberton Statue

Minnesota

VICKSBURG

Davis Statue

Texas

Memorial Arch

Alabama

Iowa

Georgia

Indiana

Rigby Statue

Please Note:
The Ohio memorials are not included on this map since Ohio has several memorials, rather than a single one. The memorials of the states of Florida, Maryland, North Carolina, South Carolina, and Virginia are outside the park boundary, hence they do not appear on this map. The sites of two observation towers, formerly located in the park are identified, although the towers themselves no longer stand. (A third tower, also now demolished, stood outside the park.)

North

0   0.1 Kilometer   0.5

0   0.1 Mile   0.5